HOW TO BECOME A ROCKSTAR GRAPHIC DESIGNER

by Casey Diggs

Publisher:
Editor: Shaquille Oliver
Cover Design: Ctdgraphicx
Graphic Design: Casey T. Diggs

Contents

The Beginning:

In this book I will share some of the key elements that I feel will guide you into becoming a *"ROCKSTAR GRAPHIC DESIGNER."* I will share a few tips, advice, and experience's that I've faced along my journey that have helped me in my career. Though this book was specifically made for graphic designers, many can view this as a guide to successfully building your career. This is more than a book for designers, but a stepping stone on how you can build your career and take your life to the next level.

Some Assumptions about Graphic Design/ designers

- Graphic designers are only meant to be in the background and never in the front of their work.
- Graphic designer should charge cheap prices for their work.
- Graphic designers aren't real artist.
- Graphic design is easy and doesn't take much effort.

Introduction

Graphic design can be one of the best and most rewarding careers one can venture into. As a designer, I can truly say that I am happy with the decision I made to venture into this career field. However, though it is rewarding, design can create many challenges and different obstacles like other careers that one may face. Graphic design is also something a person does not wake up one morning and decide to do. Just because you are creative and innovative mean that you are a designer. Design may come in many different forms, but one thing I learned about being a graphic designer is that you must have passion, dedication and a desire to think beyond ones imagination. Always dream big and see a bigger picture in yourself and in your design.

As a child, my parents Wallace & Tichina Diggs discovered this passion within me before I knew what a graphic designer was. She said, "This is a gift that was given to you by God", and in return I use it to express myself and encourage others to do the same. This gift was not designed for one person, but instead designed for multiple people to seek out a way of expressing art to the world. A good friend of mine stated that "my hands are not my hands, but these are the hands of God working through me." At that moment, that feeling gave me a sense of commitment to inspire individuals to continue to seek out their passion and drive their vision to reality. My mission in life was to design. It was a great journey to get to this point in life as choosing graphic design as my career, and I truly feel blessed.

CTDGRAPHICX

Part 1: UNDERSTANDING THE BUSINESS

Building Your Brand

How to go from being a freelance graphic designer to an actual brand

As a beginner or someone getting into the field of design, you may or may not have a company or LLC as yet, its common. This is just the start of you building your brand. It is important to start to establish yourself in your field, and use your name to your advantage. Invent yourself, use your name as your brand. Why your name? Because your name is something that you want people to remember. It is something that you want, when someone looks at a design you created, it is identified. Always market your brand name to your audience, because one day your name will be said across the world.

Next you will take your name and create a signature logo. A logo creation does not have to be fancy, or "extra" just yet. But something simple that catches the eyes of your audience, that is readable. This will be used to stamp on all your work/ creations. Having a readable signature is very important because you want your audience to know exactly who created the image, and create a sense of recognition. Eventually as your name is well known, you can create a sense of personality with your logo, but for now; let's keep it simple. In creating your logo, you can add the option of placing your website underneath for easy access and credit. For beginners, you may not have a website just yet. However, in due time; placing your website underneath will trace the work you created back to you and help establish your brand name and successfully build a "buzz" for your name.

Marketing

After your logo is created, start marketing it. Promote your logo and create a following for yourself. Create a target audience and market to that audience. Begin to establish yourself with different people to get your name across. Use sample designs to showcase your work. Utilize all aspects of social media and promote yourself.

Take things to the next level, create a logo shirt design. By placing your logo on a t-shirt, you are signifying your brand. The more you wear your shirt, the more promotion you give yourself and most importantly, the promotion is FREE! After you have your shirt, you can get a professional photoshoot done showcasing your logo t-shirt. A photoshoot of yourself is very important, for you to establish yourself and your brand. For clients, they want to see the person behind the computer and know exactly who is designing. Your logo is not the only thing to market, you as a person must market yourself because your logo is your brand and your brand is you! You may hear that it is not necessary or important for you to show your face, show your work; you're a designer, what does it matter? That's wrong! Don't let others discourage you from building your brand. I'm telling you to show your face because YOU ARE YOUR BRAND. If you personally do not want to show your face use different options or methods. As a graphic designer you can be very creative in the way you show yourself. You can use a digital cartoon photo of yourself created. One way or the other the client needs to be able to have some type of idea of what you look like. This will make them more comfortable doing business with you. After all, who wants to do business with a mysterious stranger?

Business Cards

Next create business card designs for yourself. You may say this is too professional and who carries around business cards these days in 2018? Nothing is ever too professional when it comes to building your success. It is important to carry at least a few hard copy business cards as well as have a saved digital copy in your phone to send to clients when you're on the go.

When designing your business cards, here are a few information you should include:

- Your Logo Design
- Your name
- Job title
- Email
- Phone number
- Photo of yourself (High quality photo.)
- Website link
- Social media links

Another method is having flyer designs created to promote yourself.

When designing your flyers, here are a few information you should include:

- Logo design
- Your name
- Job title (Graphic Designer)
- Email address
- Phone number
- Photo of yourself (high quality photo of yourself only)
- Prices
- Social media links

Pricing Matters

Pricing your service is a very important factor in the industry of design. For multiple reasons, this can determine your value of your design/work, show your experience, and show the amount of time you place into what you do and how you potentially do it.

One thing I always like to keep in mind is that, "your time is money." A very old cliché phrase that everyone says but may not truly understand the definite meaning of. For example, every designer needs and deserves to be paid for any work they present to a client. Depending on the project, it may take more time than others; making it time consuming. But despite that, you want to make sure you are compensated the correct price for the time and effort you've spent. You must understand that you may have to turn down jobs just to complete a task or project. Keeping in mind that you are losing a job just to maintain another. This does not mean to over price a client because of the extensivity of the current job. However, you should be able to conclude a reasonable price that makes you feel that your time was allocated within that job.

Logo Design Pricing

Designers cheat and cut themselves short in the design industry based on one factor, not understanding how to price their work. A few years back, I found that Graphic Artist starting price for a logo design started at roughly $200. Over the years, as many people joined the industry, it decreased to a starting price of $50. That's a big jump, but the market is growing so the competition is high. This does not mean to be discouraged, it just means you now have to be more creative.

Today, there are designers charging between $5 - $15 per logo design. From a $200 charge coming down to $5. This concerns me of the quality of work and the goal you wish to achieve for that price. As a designer, do not be afraid to sell your work to the price of your worth. On the other hand, I understand that many designers want to build their cliental and see that if I charge low, I will increase my business. Pricing matters, if you are worried about building a good cliental; you must price correctly to attract your consumers. This is a major marketing tactic that is universal. Research your market and view some of the best designers and their pricing compared to some of the worst and their pricing. This will definitely help you in finding the appropriate pricing for your work. Always remember that your brand is what you make of it and how you price it will determine the wealth of it.

You will always have "CHEAP CLIENTS." Those are the ones that want a design quick, fast, easy and FREE! They may love the work you give, but do not want to pay the price you give them. So the $5 - $15 design price may work for them. If they can get it for free, that's even better for them. With pricing your designs this low, you will attract cheap clients. This will also place you in the lane of "CHEAP WORK." This is work that is rushed and easy to come by. Your work may be worth $200 but because you price it so low, you will be attracting cheap clients.

Another point of pricing your designs so low is, the attraction of clients in general. This may seem like the best thing to ever happen to you, you've gotten an unlimited supply of clients sending you messages, emails, phone calls, etc. This is great, however now you have individuals wanting and waiting for a design. Many do not know the details of how this business really work. As a client, it is natural for them to think that you are a magician in Photoshop and with the raise of the magic wand the design is completed, WRONG. Your clients will begin to think that after one (1) hour, the design will be completed. Some clients may think that after twenty-four (24) hours, their design should be completed, WRONG AGAIN. With this misconception, it creates a need to rush just to keep the clients happy or a threat to demand a refund because the work was not produced to the time in which it was requested.

Pricing helps you as a designer to limit your cliental to people that know that for the price they are paying, requires time and effort to give them the quality of work they requested. Easy money, gives you an easy and quick job. Nothing in life is free, so don't expect quality work to be free and do not price your work for easy pay. One thing to remember is that, once an order is placed/ submitted and paid for, you have to create. Designing isn't like selling clothes, you do not need one thousand (1,000) orders to make money. Look at it this way, you can charge $15.00 for a logo and make 20 sales to earn a profit of $300. You can also charge $200 for a logo and get 3 clients to make a profit of $600. In the second option, you have doubled in your revenue and made $300 more than what you initially charged. Trust me when I say that it is not impossible to sell at those prices, especially if you're putting out high quality work. I will recommend when pricing logos, never make them a solid price. From my viewpoint, you can give packages so that they can have options. This gives a sense of sensitivity and comfortability to a client. Everyone loves options compared to one solid price to take or leave. This method also sets you apart from other designers that doesn't give a variety within their pricing.

Here are a few package options and ideas you can use to start your pricing.

EXAMPLE PACKAGES

LOGO DESIGNS

PACKAGE 1:

WORD TEXT LOGO DESIGN …….................................... $65

File Type includes: JPEG, PNG & PDF

This package comes with three (3) free revisions of your choice.

PACKAGE 2:

ADVANCED LOGO DESIGN …….................................... $110

File Type includes: JPEG, PNG & PDF

This package comes with three (3) free revisions of your choice.

PACKAGE 3:

EXCLUSIVE LOGO DESIGN …….................................... $200

File Type includes: JPEG, PNG & PDF

This package comes with three (3) free revisions of your choice.

Note: Never disclose your PSD file in a sale. To avoid copywriting.

After a client has used up all three (3) of their free revises, you may charge an additional fee such as example: $20 per revise. Make sure to inform the client of this so that it will not come as a shock factor or blind sight to them. This also protects you and your brand in the end if they decide to refer you or say that they were not notified or informed of this before submitting their order.

Note: Do not be scared to charge these prices. Put quality into your work and charge what you are worth.

Just as well as the value of a logo design, you may refer that information to flyer designs. Flyer designs in the past gave prices of $95. Today, designers are charging $25 and charging $60 to print up to 500 flyers for a total of $85 for a complete package. Sounds great doesn't it? As wonderful as this may sound, do not cheat yourself off your own worth. Do not let your printing company charge more than your design. Put value in your work because you worked hard to give the client exactly what they want and need. Respect your design and price correctly.

It is also important to understand that there will be clients that will approach you with request with a payment idea of $25 for a design. As the designer, you must set your marketing tactics and find ways to make your profit that increases your revenue. How much money will it cost to produce, and how much time will it take. This method will help you price your flyers accordingly considering printing and design. At this time, this is the only time it would seem fit for you to decrease your pricing. Inform your clients of your flyer design prices, then add that you have a package that includes printing and at what price. When offering print services you can decrease your price because you are making up the other portion of money through printing.

In a brief summary, the proper pricing for a print size flyer design should be approximately $60 for a front portion only and between the ranges of $75 - $85 for the front and back design. You may also charge a social media flyer design for a starting price at $45. Your pricing is your discretion, but it will determine your success and credibility.

Mixtape Covers:

Designing Mixtape Covers can truly be one of the most troubling type of designs on the financial side. It is troubling because you have to be very detailed on how you create the design and it requires little pay for completion. In the grand scheme of the music industry, you notice a lot of people trying to get into it, and some are successful and some are not. In knowing this, you have to know how to play the game and benefit with your creation. You may find a lot of talented upcoming artist that want something affordable and won't hurt their pockets as they try to make their pockets grow.

This does not mean lower your price to accommodate them. At the end of the day, you must realize that just like they are trying to brand and market themselves, you are also. You have a business and you should not need to take pity on a person because they are just starting out. So let's talk business. In the business aspect of charging for a mixtape cover design, you may want to charge around the range of $45 for the front cover only and $75 for both the front and back. These prices gives you and. your client an idea of how you pricing will work for the appropriate quality and time offered.

Banners:

Banners consist of art that can be displayed within an office, tables for promotion, outside signs, etc. Many businesses use banners for different types of promotion. From experience, a client will always look for the cheapest way to get a banner design because they feel as if it will take no more than 30 minutes to create magic and give them the quality that they want. This goes back to understanding the industry.

However, quality work comes with a time and price. The asking price that I have normally received were around $30 - $40 without prints. But this does not factor in the amount of things the clients want. You must remember that design takes time and certain aspects that are requested are not just available upon request. Therefor you as a designer should take control of this scenario and illustrate that, "I understand that you want a banner design without prints for this amount, however..." and you may continue with your charging price based on their request. Do not let the client dictate your pricing.

An appropriate pricing for a banner design can range between $80 - $100 based on the time it takes, the design requested and the type of banner needed. In retrospect of this information, you also want to factor in printing. Though the client may not need your printing services, you want to create the appropriate size for the banner to avoid issues for printing. Knowing your size for all design images is very important. Although you not printing it you going to have to make your banner size very large so it want look pixelated. This in some cases will cause your computer to maybe run a little bit slow, so you need to charge like $80 to $100.

Business Card Designs:

One of the most important things that you will ever need in your career. Many will come and ask for this. With designing this, there are two options available for you.

Option I

You may charge a one set fee of $50 that includes the front only and another set fee of $75 for the front and the back designed. The reason for splitting each design charge is to give a variety and separate your time. Designing as you've read throughout each section takes time. Though a business card is very simple, it is very beneficial to your brand and it is something that you will use for a lifetime. Therefore you must get it correct the first time around.

Option II

You may charge a fee at $85 for both front and back.

For business card designs you can do this two ways. You can charge a one set fee for front only and another for front and back which I would set at $50 for front only and $75 front and back.

The second way is to just charge a one set fee at $85, however I will say I see allot of artist make more sells when they give the client an option.

Cartoon Photos:

When it comes time for making cartoon photos you are now crossing over into the illustration side of things. You need to base your price on timing. Understand people are not going to no $100 for a cartoon photo just to post as their default on social media. They will however pay over $100 for a cartoon logo design because of the value in it. With cartoon photos I suggest if you trying to make money with it stay away from doing cartoon defaults and try to incorporate into using for logos and if you can also use it for mixtape covers also, and you can now up sell on your mixtape covers.

LIFE
SUCCESS
HAPPY
Think B4 You Act
GIFTED
AMBITOUS
DRIVE
HUMBLE
BLESSED
STRONG
JOYFUL
BRIGHT
SMART
POWERFUL
NEVER LOOK BACK
ALWAY LOOK
FORWARD
JOY

Setting Contracts

One of the main reasons designers fall short or run into problems in this industry is because there was never a set contract given. It is very important that before you do anything, you present to your client a contract that details your services, an agreement and the type of service requested and offered.

Throughout my career, I've struggled with doing this because as a self-taught person in this profession; you just don't know these things. I've given benefit of doubts to many individuals and sadly I've been burned by doing this. You never want to feel as if you are being used or taken advantage of for your art or craft.

Along with designing, you will be exposed to different clients that allow your network to grow. There is potential to be seen by various amount of different people throughout the world within different industries. Graphic design is one of the few occupations that can get you noticed in different aspects of different industries. Therefore you will definitely need to protect yourself as well as your clients by producing a set contract before providing any work needed. The contract is what will make you and the other party involved have a clear understanding and agreement of what to expect, the type of work you will provide, what you will need from them to get the job complete and other contributions and details. Without a contract or written agreement, nothing is secure and things can change at any moment of the transaction. Never go by verbal communication. An example can include: if you offer a client three (3) revisions on a design, but there is no documentation that states this information, a client can come back and state that this was never communicated or informed. Even if there was a verbal communication of this information, a client can state that there is no recollection of this information therefore this transaction cannot be completed. You have then lost your stand on the matter, and run into a big problem with a client that can potentially harm your business.

This may also include refunds being subjected to the client, or additional work that could've been avoided if there were documents set in place with appropriate signatures and copies for references.

The highlight that really amazes people with being a designer is the opportunity to work with different celebrities. As a celebrity graphic designer, I can understand the excitement. However, this does not make them any different than regular people. No matter who you are, your business must remain the same for everyone. A contract will definitely make your business more professional and creditable to clients.

From experience, I too was amazed and truly blessed working with the amazing people that requested my services. However, though individuals may have different status in life, this does not change their characteristics. A person's true character will always come out in some way that will make you see what it's truly like to work with different types of people. Nonetheless, I was given the opportunity to work with a reality star on a major network and made verbal agreements assuming that they would stay true to their word. I believed in people as they believed in me. As a designer, you would always want for people to believe in you, however this does not mean to be naive in the pursuit of those beliefs. Never mistake belief for being taken advantage of.

The agreement that was set in place was to provide "FREE graphic designs for their business, and in return I would be featured on their segment of their show.

Like any upcoming designer, this is huge. You want your hard work to be noticed and be paid off with a sense of accomplishment. I agreed to this transaction verbally and proceeded to take a trip to Atlanta with my own expenses. I met a few cast members, and did a few filming with the client as stated in the verbal agreement. In return I gave her the graphics, free of charge as she proceeded to post the work on social media and other means to market without giving credit to me as the designer. Rule number 1 within designing or accepting design work, you should always give credit to the designer to show gratitude and appreciation. This is a huge disrespect to a designer when you cut, remove or hide their signature or ignore crediting them for their work.

In the end, as the show aired, my work was displayed but I was not. Credit was not given, and I was not acknowledged. When I asked the client about the agreement, it was said that he/she had no idea of what happened, and nobody knew until the day of the release. Then in response to that, I was informed that there was no written contract to conclude the agreements of our transaction, therefore I was owed nothing.

At that moment, I knew the difference between a verbal contract and a written contract. That written contract would've protected myself against any information stated, my work would've not been released without the proper channel through me and compensation. That contract would've created a legal bind between myself, the client and the network for the improper release of my work without my permission. Although the show is cancelled due to other situations not pertaining to me, it was indeed a learning experience for myself and a better understanding of the business and its industry. However, my suggestion to avoid any of this is to always have a contract and keep copies of that contract because you never know when you might need it.

You may note that contracts may be a hassle or a challenge to create, however there are many different options for you to go through to complete this. Utilize google to find different samples and examples of contracts, along with using a site called, fiverr.com and use someone with excellent experience that will create a contract for you at a very reasonable price.

TIP: When creating contracts, create an online and a printed copy where you can sign electronically and psychically.

NEVER BE SCARED
TO SHOW THE WORLD
THE TALENT GOD
BLESSED YOU WITH!!!

Provide logical turnaround times

Providing logical turnaround times simply means to manage your time wisely and efficiently. Do not over exert yourself into thinking that you can complete 50 designs in one hour. That is not logical if you want creativity, preciseness and other meanings that partake within the design process.

However, it is possible that you will run into many clients that want fast turnaround time. A client will put an order in at 3:00 PM and expect it to be completed by 4:00 PM. Logically, if you have nothing to do and you're simply sitting around and waiting for a client, this may be possible. This is taking into consideration the design that is needed. However, if you factor in other clients as well as other obligations that you have prior commitments to, this would be an issue.

To eliminate all unnecessary aspects of this, you must first remember that you are one person and can only do so much at that time. Designing requires time, commitment and creativity. As designers we do in fact need a break, we do get tired, and we do need to rejuvenate our creative process to continue on with our work. It has taken me a great deal of stress to understand this factor, as to why I am stressing this out. As an entrepreneur within this design field, you will always want to do your best, perfect your craft and continue to excel with your work. The more clients, the better you would think. I would take on as many clients as possible and agree to have the work completed by the next day. This created chaos within my schedule because of the amount of work load that I committed to myself. Orders upon orders would come in, and it was almost impossible for me to say no to any client.

In the end, I learned a valuable lesson. You cannot over work yourself and you cannot be superman to clients that need their work in the time that you gave them. With learning this process, I lost a numerous amount of clients that viewed this as inconsiderate and unprofessional. I had given them an unrealistic time frame that gave them unrealistic hope that they would get their product at the time I stated.

When I fell behind in my work, that caused the clients to fall behind on their vision or their business on what they were trying to get completed. If I had given them a reliable time frame in which we both could've worked towards to finding a proper solution, this would've set a lower expectation and allowed time to work any issues with timing.

So always remember that time is money and you don't want to lose out on it. It's always better to be upfront with the client and give them realistic time frames rather than to state something unrealistic and postpone a transaction that in the end will cause multiple issues.

The best way how to avoid getting into this situation is to go by the amount of orders you usually get in a week and how long it will take you to design them. For example if you get a high volume of orders weekly, allow your turnaround time to be 7 - 14 business days. Do not over exert yourself by utilizing the weekend times within your schedule. Designers do need a break and do need to set a schedule for free time to keep your creativity flowing. If a client needs the design at an earlier stage, you may charge a rush fee. This postpones other designs that you may have had in your query and pushes this up further. With the postponed designs, the time frame of 7 - 14 business days works because it gives a very large time range for you to allow a few rush orders to be completed if necessary. Remember even when it comes to the rush fee jobs, only take on how many you can complete in that time. Your rush job time will be shorter than 7 - 14 business days and maybe about 3 - 5 business days or you can extend it to 6. With taking on a rush order, do not take on 20 rush jobs for the same turnaround time. Remember that you also have prior jobs that you have with only 7 - 14 business days. Doing this will put you right back in the situation you previously were in. You must have a cut off time frame and limit. Know your limit and know how to control your time.

To conclude, set a schedule and utilize different guidelines for your turnaround times to avoid falling behind on your work.

THE TALENT IS ALREADY IN YOU
NOW ALL YOU HAVE TO DO IS LET IT OUT!

GRAPHIC DESIGNER WEB DESIGNER PHOTOGRAPHER

Setting Business Hours

Graphic designer's listen to me when I say that you must have a set business hours of operation. I get it this your passion, this what you love to do, but you also are a human that needs to rest, rebuild and rejuvenate your energy and creativity.

It is important to establish rules for your business and hours of operation. At no point is it appropriate for a client to be calling you at 1 AM to discuss business. This is the act of unprofessionalism and disrespect to your personal life. You must set that boundary limit to every client, to please respect these rules.

If a client refuses to abide by these rules, then that is not the client you would want to continue to conduct business with. Your time and your health is very important in this industry. There is no need for you to jeopardize your mental health for a client. This rule is simply a common courtesy towards a person and should be respected under every given circumstance. Walmart may be 24/7 but you do not have to be. If you chose to design around those hours, that is entirely up to you. However, set your time schedules for business and go by them.

LOGO DESIGN INSPIRATION

Finding your "Nitch"

Graphic design is different, it has many different aspects and avenues that it can go into. There designers that are skilled in adobe illustrator, adobe Photoshop, the entire adobe suite or even other software that can give you similar results. There are also designers that are strictly t-shirt designers, illustration designers or simply logo or flyer designers. You can restrict yourself in any way you want to focus and perfect that "nitch" of design. This does not make you less of a designer despite what anyone may say. Some people are skilled in every aspect of graphic design but simply prefer to focus on one aspect because it is what they are comfortable with.

When finding your "nitch", you must first find what aspect of design you are most comfortable with and enjoy creating. With finding your comfortability this creates an urge to create perfection. You want to find something that gives you a peace of mind and gives you pleasure when you do it. What brings out your creativity and after creating it, gives you a sense of accomplishment that shows your pride. This can become your "nitch" that will advance you to the next level of your success. For myself, my "nitch" was in logo designs. Logo designs were something I enjoyed creating due to my love for creating an identity for someone. The idea of introducing a brand for the first time to a viewer gave me a sense of accomplishment that I helped bring a person's vision to life.

When I realized designing logos was something I enjoyed, I decided to expand on this and develop a plan of action. I wanted to make this my career and help people reach their goals creatively. I started this by offering $25 for each logo design just to get my name floating. Logo designs will always be my "nitch" and something that I continue practicing and working hard to improve on because designing will always be my passion. If I ever had a rough day, I would always pull up my laptop and start designing a logo. Logos are fun, creative and make me a graphic designer.

So when you find your "nitch," always run back to it and perfect it. No matter what you design, your "nitch" will always be your safe haven. If you select yourself to be a certain type of designer, research your type, find your "nitch" and keep going.

WWW.CTDGRAPHICX.COM

Part 2: THE TOOLS

Website design \ Online Portfolio

As a graphic designer if you want clients to take you serious you must have a website. Clients will not work with you if you do not have anything to prove what you say you can do. A website builds connection, creativity and establishes credibility. These are key factors that will make you in this industry. I know a lot of designers use social media as their portfolio and that is a great way to network, but that is not the completion of the designer process. Your website is your online design portfolio in which a client can book you and review your work. Instagram, Twitter and other social media outlets can only take you so far. A website can keep your work and display it further than what social media can do. You will be amazed at how your sales will increase once you have your own website or online portfolio. Your website is going to become your office. If you don't have one get one.

The first thing you will need to do to get your website going is to establish your domain or hosting website. A popular and creditable site would be www.Godaddy.com. On this site, you can create and buy your domain name which should be roughly under $20. This is an important investment that you will need to establish yourself in this business.

What is your domain name? Your domain name is the website link people will type in to a search engine and find you. Example: www.ctdgraphicx.com. Most website builders will provide you with a sub-domain, however that is something you want to stay away from using. Sub-domains are unnecessary ways for your sites hosting name to be shown so that everyone can know where your site was built. Hidden fact, this may also make your views see you less of a designer with building your own domain as they compare you to other designers. You may either look cheap, or look like you took an easy approach to creating a website compared to someone else that takes a different route. For example, there are many designers that prefer to craft their website through strict and precise coding and there are others that just want a website to host their designs. It does not make you less of a designer, but this is a simple preference. This method is also helpful for individuals that want to focus more on graphic design compared to web design. If graphic design is more of your strong point, you will still need a website, however; your website does not have to be as detailed because you are not selling to your audience that aspect of design. You are simply showcasing a portfolio website. In the end, if you are not going to take your brand serious; you can't expect anyone else to.

For starters, I would recommend you compare different website building sites to engage in to see what gives you enough creative space to build your site. Establish your own comfortability with a site, and get to designing.

For someone who has never created a website before, this can create a challenge and may cause frustration. However, the key to this field is to never give up, design takes time and effort. On average, a website if you are just getting started may take you a few days before full completion. So never feel that your work is taking forever. If you are a perfectionist, it may take a little longer. Do not let that discourage you from creating your platform.

One of the easiest ways to give up is to hire a web designer as you are venturing into graphic design. You may feel that it's not your level of expertise. As a designer, I would encourage you to not give up and keep working on your project. Use your resources to your advantage. Watch videos and other tutorials on how you can design a website or webpage. It may look hard now, but in the end it will become easy and will be worth it.

Before
After
GRAPHIC DESIGNS I CREATED FOR LOVELY MIMI FROM VH1 HIT
REALITY TV SHOW "LOVE AND HIP HOP ATLANTA"
LOVELY MIMI
POP BIT OF MI
1. INTRO
2. GO LIVE
3. STRIP FT. KOLTEN PERINE
4. HIGH
5. INTERLUDE
6. LIFE OF MI
7. PRIME TIME FT. 5IVE & KOLTEN PERINE (BONUS)

Be Confident Not Cocky

As a graphic designer understand you need to have confidence in yourself and in your work. Clients will come to you, expecting something of high quality to represent their brand to help their business to grow. It is your job as a designer to make their vision come to life and expand on it. Confidence will always be key in the success of your business. When you act confident, you will eventually become confident. Always show your confidence to make your clients feel comfortable.

Never mistake confidence with "cockiness." Over exaggerating your confidence can come across as arrogant and disrespectful. You never want to make a client feel that you are inferior towards them or their idea is not worthy enough to be accepted by yourself. No job is too good or too bad to accept. You must always treat all clients equally to avoid favoritism and disrespect.

One thing that I've learned is that you can be high one day, but if you do not exert humbleness and appreciation for what you have, you can be brought right back down. What you have will always be a blessing, and that's something you should never forget. Always remain humble because you can have it all one minute and loose it all the next. You are not the only graphic design artist in this industry, so do not ever feel like you are irreplaceable.

DIGITAL SMUDGE PAINTING

The artwork you see here was for Momma Dee Known as the mother of famous rapper "LIL SCRAPPY" and from Vh1 hit reality tv show "LOVE AND HIP HOP". As you see both stars expressed their thoughts on the artwork I created for them through social media.

Patience Produces Structure

Having patience with design

If you guys haven't learned by now reading this book I'm going to give you the real deal straight forward no sugar coating the truth. In this journey to become a rockstar graphic designer, you must have patience. Everything involving graphic design, which includes getting clients and creating a connection with these clients will require patience, time and commitment.

This right here will determine if you have it to not only be a graphic designer but a successful business owner. Sometimes you have to ask yourself... "Do you have the patients to work hard and put in the work to build your brand up?" "Do you have the patients to learn more to enhance your craft?"

Without patience you won't make it in this business. Designing is not something you can rush through and become a rockstar at it. There are some designers that can design quickly, and there are others that require time. Coming into this industry at first, you will need to have patience and give yourself that time. You never want to rush your craft, so give yourself that necessary time to complete the task to perfection and your liking. Remember, it's your name on it at the end of the day.

Having Patients with clients

Everyone does not know the industry and what it takes to create a design. This is not an issue, however there are some clients that can be very difficult and will make your life a little stressful because of the lack of knowledge of what is put into graphic design.

Clients for starters may come to you not understanding what they want and how they want it. It is your job to coach and guide them into the direction of what they may possibly want. Provide examples, suggestions or ideas that you may notice that can help them with a decision. Ask appropriate questions to get them comfortable and make them feel that they had an active part in helping you understand their vision of design. Communication will give them the sense of commitment to the craft along with patience and comfortability.

You may run into a client that will ask you the same question several times, but in a different format. Do not let this be the discourager that they are not understanding you. It simply means that they are trying to get an understanding but see that their question though it is worded differently, might mean something different. Along with the act of questions, you may run into clients that will constantly check up on you, and give a new idea or ask a question for clarification and understanding. It is your job to get the client comfortable and reassure them of what you are doing along with your process.

Some clients may even contact you in reference to something that you have that's self-explanatory. Re-stating the statement gives the client a sense of security that helps them. You must have continued patience when dealing with clients. Always remain calm, courteous and professional when dealing with any situation involving a client. This is a true aspect of a designer.

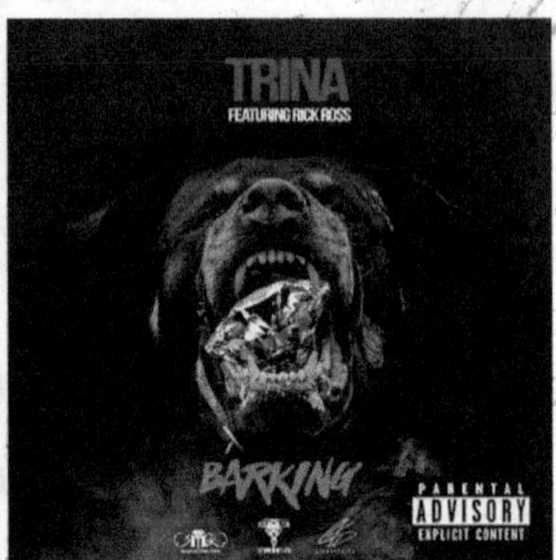

MIXTAPE COVER
DESIGNS

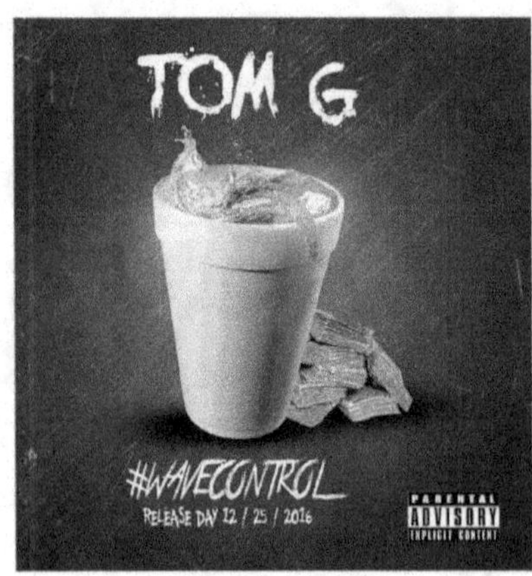

Believe in your success

If I don't know anything else, I know that starting off as a graphic designer requires a lot of will power, commitment and patience. You don't want to ever give up and lose hope. As you start off, you have to understand that it will not be easy. As i stated before, you must have patience, everything takes time and building your network will require a lot of time, patience and commitment. With all the added work, this can become stressful and discouraging. You want the success, but you have to put in the work. Your business will not grow over night, and you will not become successful overnight.

As an entrepreneur, you may feel that if you're not making money, you're not doing anything productive and things aren't going the way you wanted it to go. Never lose hope and say that you are in the wrong career field or something is wrong with you and your work. Always keep practicing and eventually your hard work will pay off. At times it will take 5, 10 or maybe 20 years for you to see how far your investment has come. Everyone's journey will be different, and you will not walk the same path way. Even if you feel like you did, your obstacles will be far different. So it is important to never lose sight of what you want for yourself and always keep your head up. Do not lose the faith that you have on yourself.

As a designer, you have to keep faith alive because without faith in yourself, you cannot expect people to have faith in you. When I first started this career path, I was not making any money, I would just design for free. There have been times where I wanted to give up, I felt I wasn't good enough and my designs were only meant to be free. I had other jobs, so money was not an issue; but it never gave me the fulfillment that I was looking for. I felt unhappy with everything that was presented in front of me. My success was only a dream, but then I looked to God for faith and guidance. I remembered that, I had a purpose; to design.

As I continued designing, there would always be thoughts of not doing something right and wondering what more can I do to gain my success. I kept feeling defeated as I constantly had thoughts about giving up, but deep down; my ambition would not let me. I always found that one strength to continue to move forward. I would think, that I would be giving up on my dream and then what? Now I can say that I'm so thankful that I didn't because of the blessings and experience that I have had.

This experience has been amazing and I would never change any part of it. As a designer, things can happen, things can change and you can be a rockstar designer.

As I conclude, always strive to be your best and be your own success story. Understand when you get into this career field that there will be people that will envy you, discourage you and push you to anger, pain and resentment but you must always remember to NEVER GIVE UP!

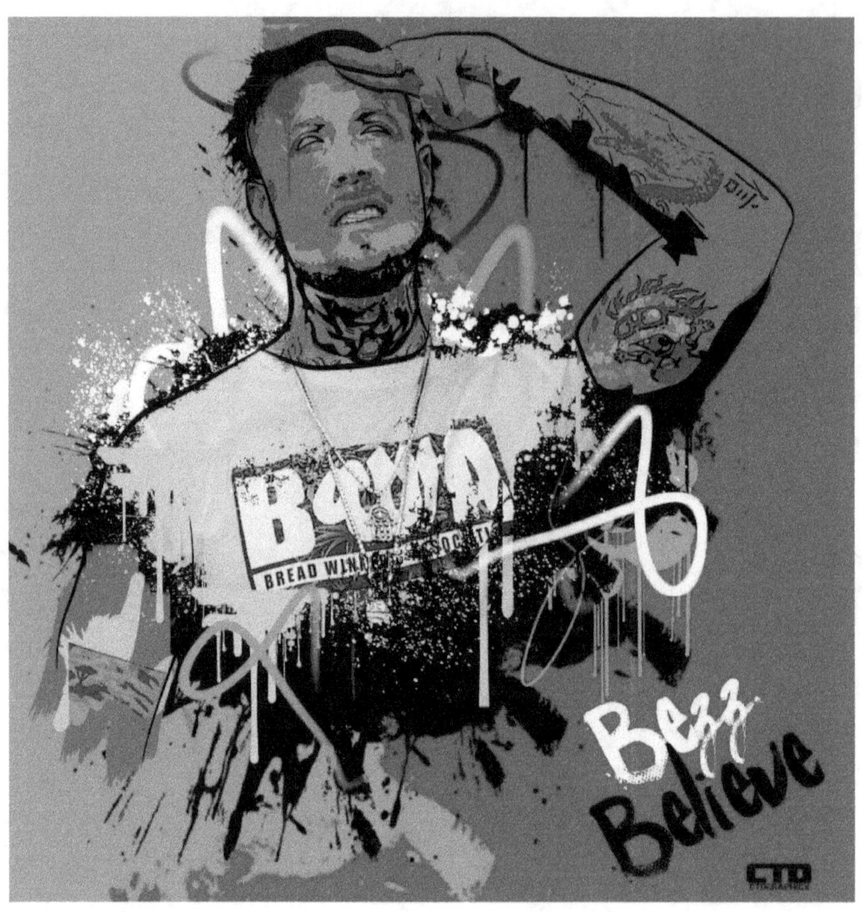
BWA
BREAD WINNERS SOCIETY
Bezz
Believe
CTD

Part 3: **THE REALITY OF IT**

Knowing your value
Service exchange for exposure

As a graphic designer we provide a service to something that everyone needs. There will be times people will approach you asking for an exchange. If you design something for them, instead of a payment; you can exchange for exposure. There is nothing wrong with wanting to get your name exposed to create more cliental. However, you must weigh the benefits of doing this. What are you benefiting from this type of exposure, will the time and effort you took in creating this design weight out the cause of non-payment for the exposure? Will your brand be impacted by this exposure or will it be brushed to the side as a simple "like on Instagram." Many may have viewers, but will those viewers pay attention to create traffic for your network.

You must also know the type of market that person is catering to. Just because they have a certain following mean that it will transfer to you because of exposure. Some people are loyal and some people may gravitate to someone else. This is a win/lose situation because it requires heavy thought and research. But remember 100K followers does not mean, work with that person for free for exposure. Research their audience because they may not show an interest in what you do. Always remember that what works for some may not work for all.

I have found myself creating graphics for exposure and sometimes it benefited me and other times it didn't. Had I known to research the demographics of these individuals, I may have been more careful. But with doing this, comes a learning experience. Do not be fooled by the following. I've worked with individuals with a following of 500k and received feedback of possibly 3 compared to working with an individual with 80k - 100k and received around 50 - 80 followers with added sales of business.

Another important rule is to know the type of exposure you want to receive. If you are being promoted on someone else's social media, be sure it is done correctly and not just put together because that person feels that they need to do it. An example is by placing a caption titled, "designed by..." with additional hashtags is not the proper way and can be overlooked. Sometimes you have to think, "will my viewers really look at this?" Most people think long and hard about a great caption that will attract their viewers. Don't put together something that will give a negative look on someone that worked hard to support you. Support in full.

In the end, exposure sometimes can be a good thing, however too many exposures will run you into doing too many favors that can potentially harm yourself and business. You do not want to bend backwards for someone that can't do the same in return for you. Also, please do not allow everyone to take advantage of you and create a trend that you will do a design for exposure. You cannot do this for everyone because everyone will think they are entitled to get something for free.

INSPIRATIONAL FLYER DESIGNS

Support System

Understand that as you grow you will encounter a lot of different people with different characteristics. As a talented artist you must weed out the people that will be there for you versus the people that won't elevate you. Remember that not everybody will have your best interest at heart. You must take notes of who to associate yourself with and who not to in this industry because there are people that will use you for convenience. I am not saying that everyone that comes to you, will treat you this way; however it is important not to mix business with pleasure. You cannot bring everyone to your work environment. This gives you a bad look of unprofessionalism.

When I first started working for a magazine company, they suggested that I sign my company under there's. This would've created a networking experience for me, however in thought; it was stating that they would basically be managing me. You may look at this as a good thing to be under a well-established company. But when you don't have the same view points, ethics and other characteristics that goes hand in hand, this will cause friction. In thought, if I were to agree to this, any work presented to me would be split between myself and the company. So in the end, I felt that they would've benefited more than myself. In some cases, this can be a great thing and in others you may feel that there are better opportunities for yourself. You are entitled to turn down offers despite an offer sounding too good to be true. The truth is had I signed under them, there is a high chance I wouldn't be where I'm at today, because that magazine company isn't in business today. You must do what feels right and comfortable for yourself.

When someone presents you an offer, you must think cautiously about the effects of accepting and declining that offer. You need to do an extensive background check on the credentials that this company has to offer, review all positive and negative aspects of the company. Research different employees and what they've done throughout the company. If this is a company that wants to manage you based on your creativity, review pass persons within the profession to get a general idea of the type of people they looked for and the benefits that were presented to them. Anyone can manage someone, but what happens after managing can make an impact to your brand. Once you do your research and you don't see anything there that will benefit you, it is natural to walk away and decline the offer.

One thing I've always said and kept with myself is, "how can you teach someone to make 1 million dollars, if you've never made it? How can you teach someone how to grow a business if your business is still pending?"

In this field of work there are a lot of opportunities that will come your way. There will be opportunities that will excite you and as you take advantage of them, you may want to include your friends. This can be a good thing or a bad thing. Your friends may be the closest thing to you, however do not mix friendship with your business. Not all the time your friendship can crossover and you can include your friend in every aspect of your career. Know the limits and set boundaries. You may have friends that think they are entitled to be there with you as you get offers. Your career may test your friendship. Be careful how you present yourself and how you handle your opportunities. The people you carry around you will set the tone of business and say a lot about you as a person.

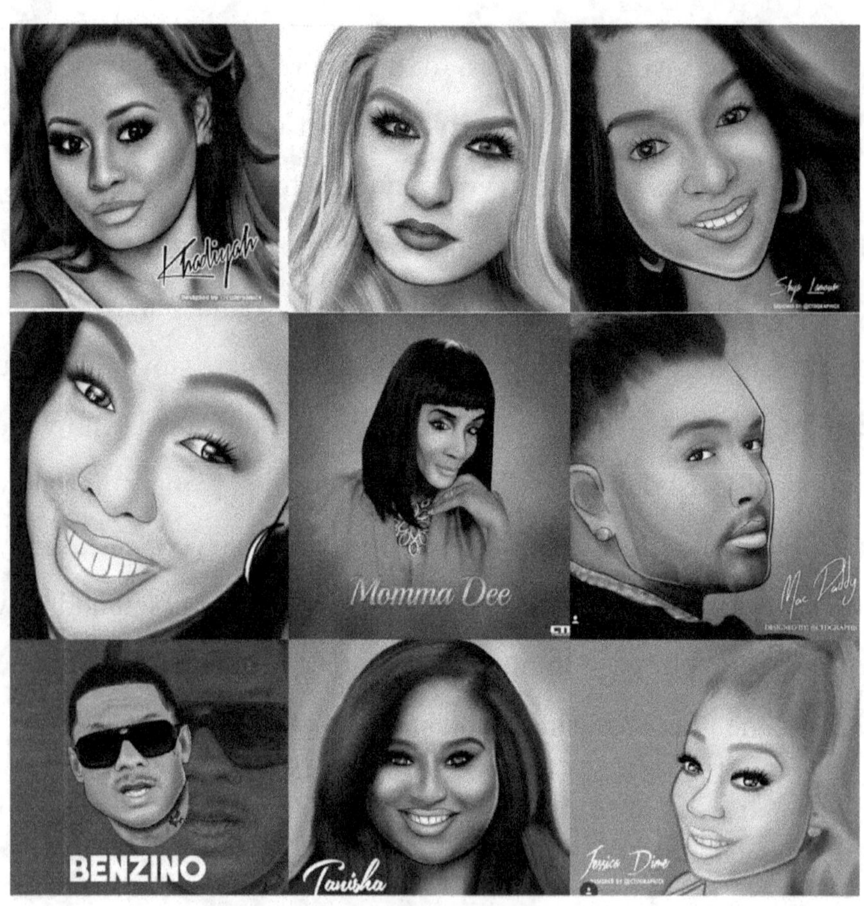

CARTOON ANIMES

Maintaining a Network to create a Net worth

One of the biggest motivators and things people may not do in this industry is support. I've seen many designers criticize, create false accusations and destroy the reputation of another designer.

Everyone has an ego, and within this industry; each individual will showcase that ego and do anything to be the best as they will claim they are. One factor of these egos may include there not being enough room for "too many designers" and there can only be one winner in this industry. This statement is very much invalid, and should not be said by anyone. Design is more than a skill, or a passion, it is a gift that anyone can possess. Never be that person that will not share your craft and help elevate a person to the next level within the industry. Do not be that person to close the door on another person because of selfishness and greed when you both can walk away with a big opportunity and advance in the industry. Always remain humble and continue to excel with your work.

Understand me, when I state that there is something unique and different in every designer that nobody can take from you. Each designer has a different way of designing, creating and expressing their vision. So who's going to steal your creativity? The door to success is open for everyone, not just one person. So if someone is blocking your pathway, find another because there's multiple but I can assure you that when theirs stops; yours will keep going.

If you're that person that's held up by greed and false statements of thinking that there's only room for one designer, I urge you to change your mindset and learn from others. Design will always be a learning experience. As designers you can always learn from one another as well teach one another. So do not stop yourself by placing a block on what you can and will do.

Uplifting is power you want to showcase. Give that power to earn that respect not just in the design world, but in the industry. More people will gravitate towards you because you are that connection that can bridge the gap in the industry. When others win, you can win too. You never know, the shoes you step on now may be the shoes you will be brushing later. I say that to say, watch who you walk over, because they just might step on your shoes while they are walking past you.

I will always pride myself in uplifting and encouraging other designers because when I came into the game, I didn't have that. That feeling of being put down by another designer and being told you'll never understand the industry will eat you inside. You never want to have that feeling of discouragement, and know that your work will never be good enough. Everyone has a dream, and designing may be your dream, but it is also someone else's. Don't close someone's door because it might fly open one day and close yours.

BUSINESS CARDS
DESIGNS INSPIRATIONS

Part 4: RESOURCES
Sites that offer free photos

Here is a freebie that you can use to gather information on where to find free photos that you can use as a designer.

As a graphic designer, it is definitely hard to find quality photos for your work. You can't just go onto google and search for an image and use it without the proper consent. You think because it's there, it's free to use. However, there are risks with using that method. Most of the time you may get away with this method, however there may be a time when you are not so lucky. This can create several different law suits against your name and your brand. So as a designer you have to be very careful with what you do and how you do it. You not only will put yourself at risk, but the client that you designed the image for at another risk.

Ways to avoid all of this is by utilizing some of these websites for free use of images. I have found these not only helpful but convenient for use. Along with these websites, you can also purchase different photos from online to use. This also protects you from law suits.

Another method that I love is that, when you simply cannot find the right image that you are looking for; you can always create it. One of the benefits of loving art is that I not only love to design, I love to create. I am a graphic designer and photographer, and when I cannot find an image that I specifically want; I create it with photography. As a designer, please do not be afraid to create your own image to use for your design work. It also saves you a lot of time when it comes to researching and finding something that suites your needs.

WEBSITES TO USE FOR FREE PHOTO IMAGES:

(Note: Please do not use and abuse this website. I do not own any rights to any of the images on any of these websites.)

www.burst.shopify.com

www.pexels.com

www.foodiesfeed.com

www.gratisography.com

www.negativespace.co

www.freestocks.org

www.picography.co

www.mmtstock.com

www.skitterphoto.com

www.lifeofpix.com

www.picjumbo.com

www.imcreator.com/free

www.mixtapepsd.com/portfolio/

STOCK PHOTO AGENCIES:

(Note: Please do not use and abuse this website. I do not own any rights to any of the images on any of these websites.)

www.istockphoto.com

us.fotolia.com

www.dreamstime.com

www.shutterstock.com

Trina
7 hrs · 🌐

Wonder were I get some of my flyers created at? Hit up
@ctdgraphicx www.ctdgraphicx.com

Sizing your designs

Knowing your sizes when it comes time for Graphic design; specially with flyers, banners, postcards, mixtapes, and etc is a very important factor. If you create a design in the wrong size when it comes time to print you can run into some serious issues and experience half of your design getting cut off.

Below I have a listing of what you should set all your sizes to be.

Postcards:
Standard: 5.47x4.21
Oversized: 8.5x5.47

Business Cards:
No Bleed Horizontal: 3.43" x 1.93"
No Bleed Vertical: 1.93"x3.43"
Bleed Horizontal: 3.54" x 2.05"
Bleed Vertical: 2.05" x 3.54"

Posters:
Small: 11.25"x17.3"
Medium: 18"x24"
Large: 24"x36"

Flyers:
4in by 6 in
5in by 7in
8in by 11in

The Beginning: How to design a background for a flyer

In this chapter you will be learning the basics step by step on how to create a background from scratch for a flyer design.

STEP 1

Open the Photoshop program. Then click on the file tab that's located in the top left corner. Select **New**..

STEP 2

Select your size dimension to 4 inch x 6 inch. Also set your resolution at 300dpi.

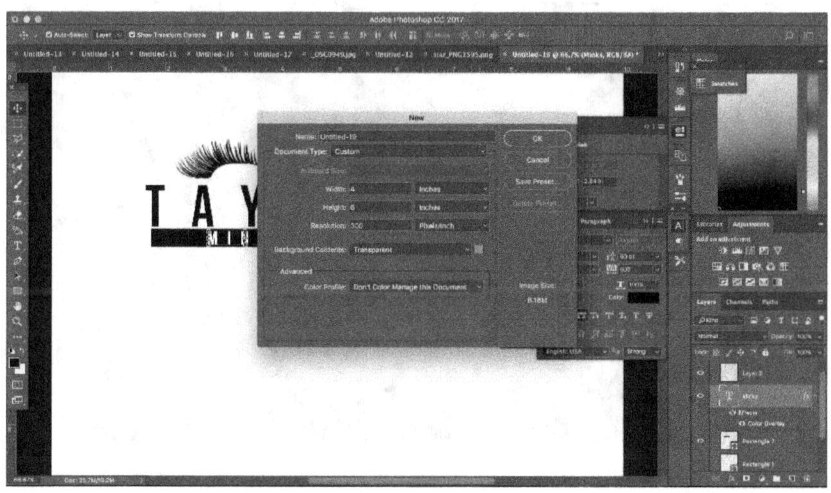

STEP 3

Go back to your menu bar and click view and scroll down to where you see rulers and select. This will help with setting up the bleeding points.

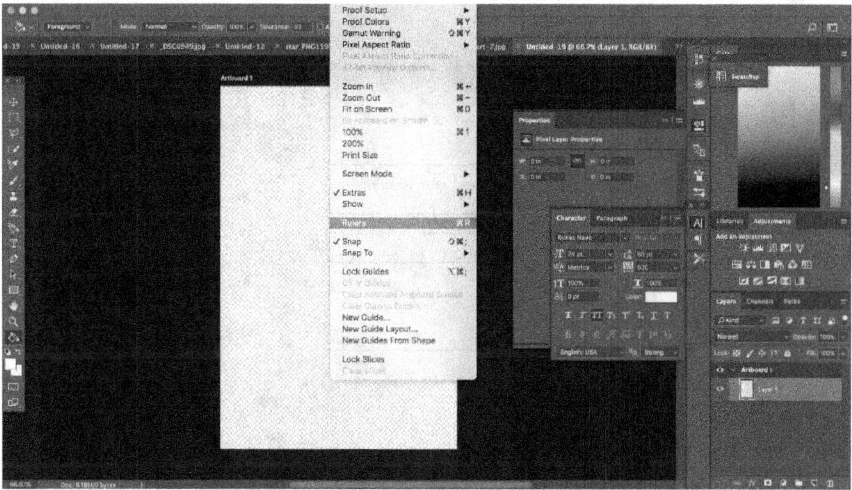

STEP 4

You're going to click on the ruler and drag the blue line down and line it up on each side your white box.

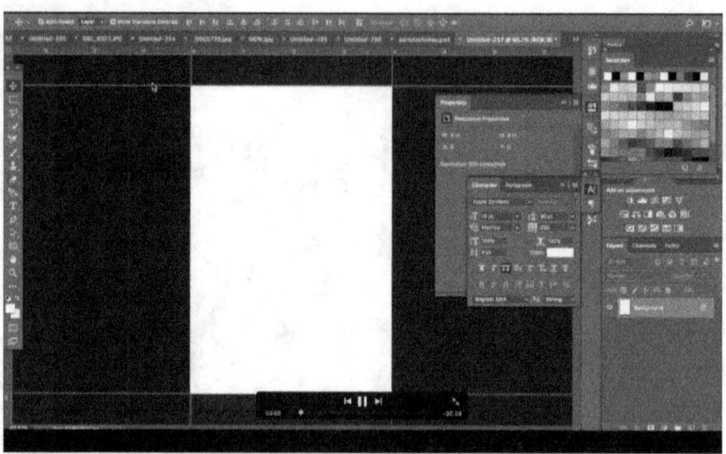

STEP 5

No we are going to go back up top and click on the image tab and go down to canvas size and click it. Next you're going to set your width and height to .25, make sure that it's done in inches as well.

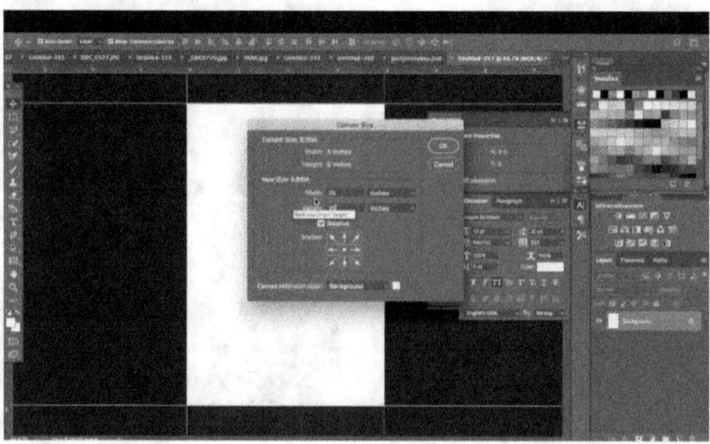

After you hit the ok button your flyer layout lines should look like the one in the image below.

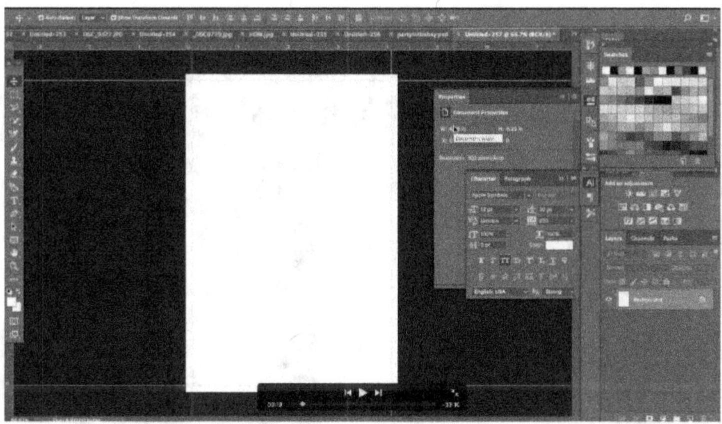

You have now completed the first few steps on setting up your flyer design before designing by adding in the bleeding points.

STEP 6

Next we are going to go into making our own background. We will first need to go create a new layer by clicking the "**Create New Layer**" button in the bottom right hand corner.

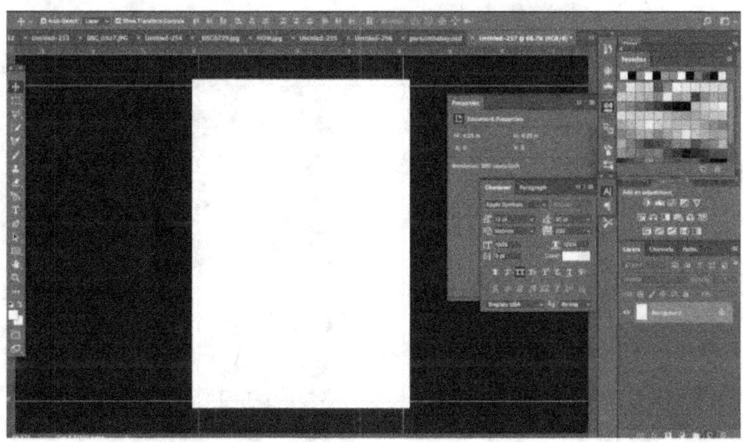

STEP 7

After that we are going to go over to out tool bar on our left hand side and click on our paint bucket tool.

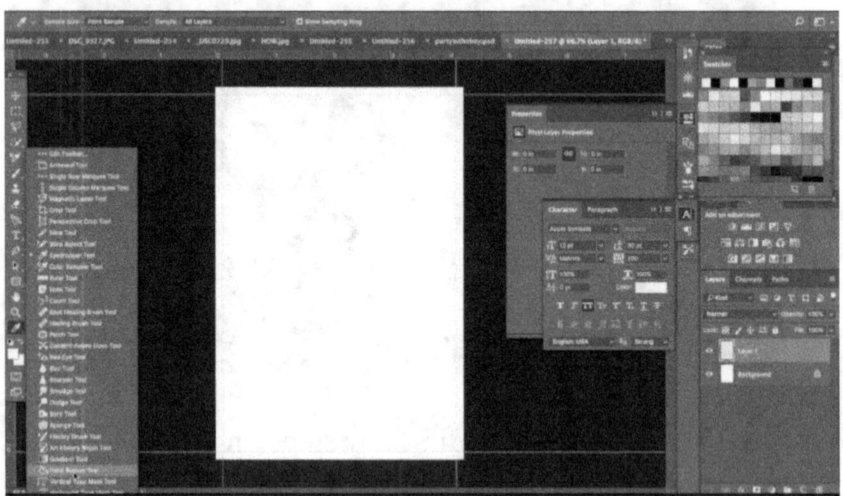

STEP 8

After that we are going to click on our color tool on our tool bar at the bottom and select Black as your color.

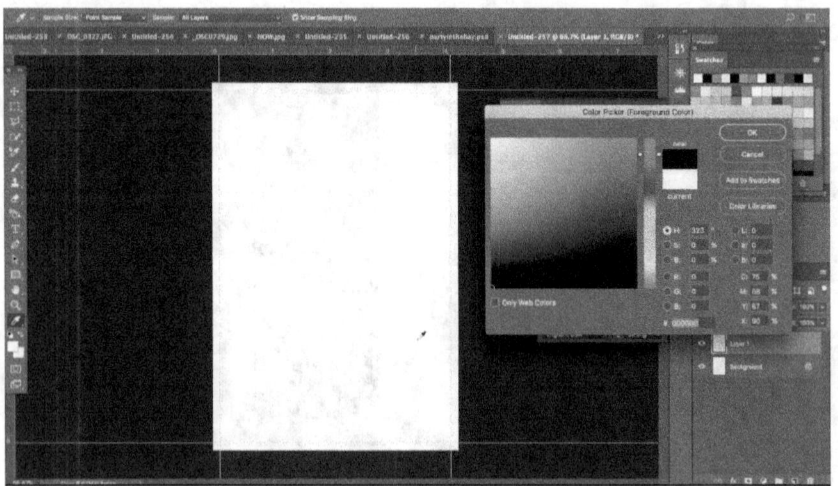

STEP 9

After that you're going to take your paint bucket and click inside your white box sure to make your whole background black. After that you're going to create another layer then go over to your tool bar and select your brush tool.

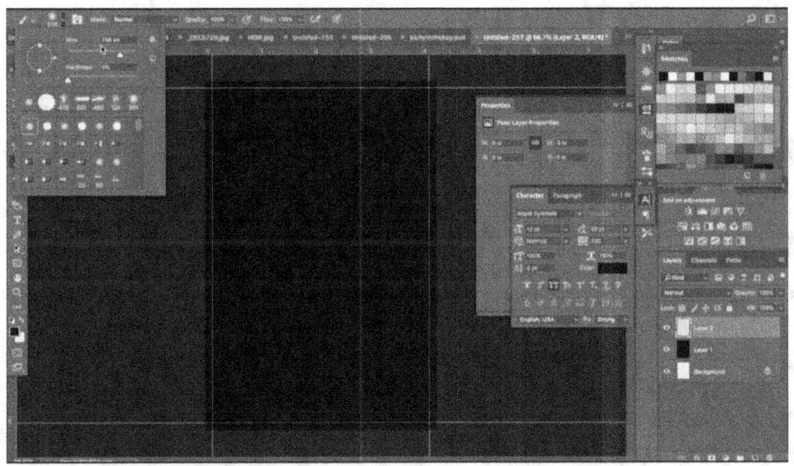

STEP 10

After you select your soft bush you're going to go back to your tool bar and select the color box and change it to pink.

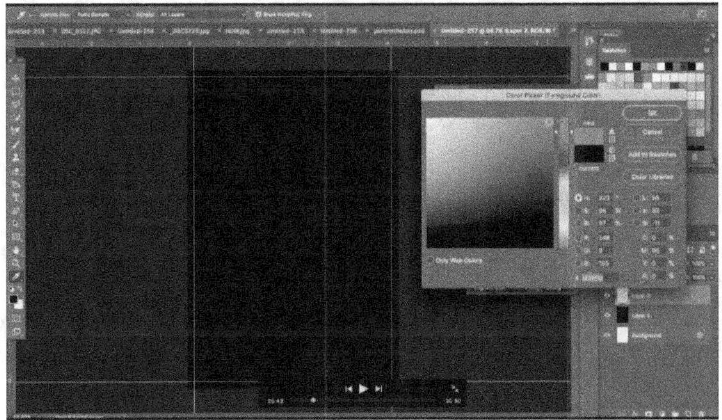

Next your will take your paint brush and place it over the black box and then click inside the black box your will see the soft pink appear. Make sure you make a new layer when doing this as you see in the picture.

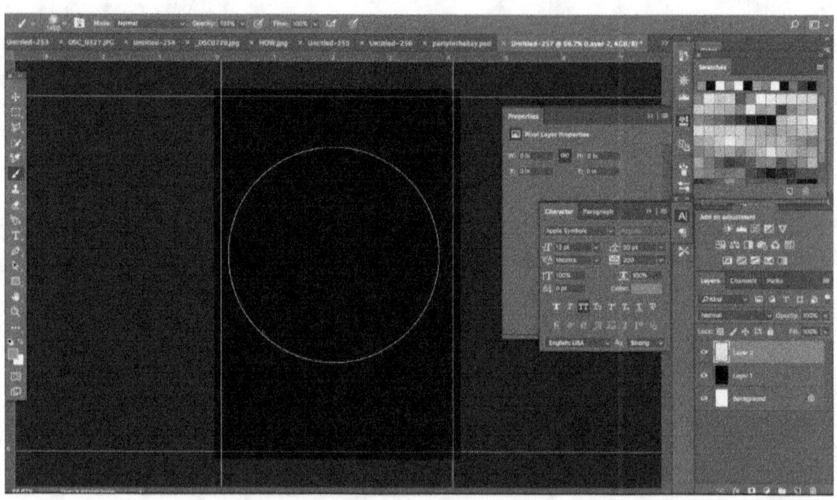

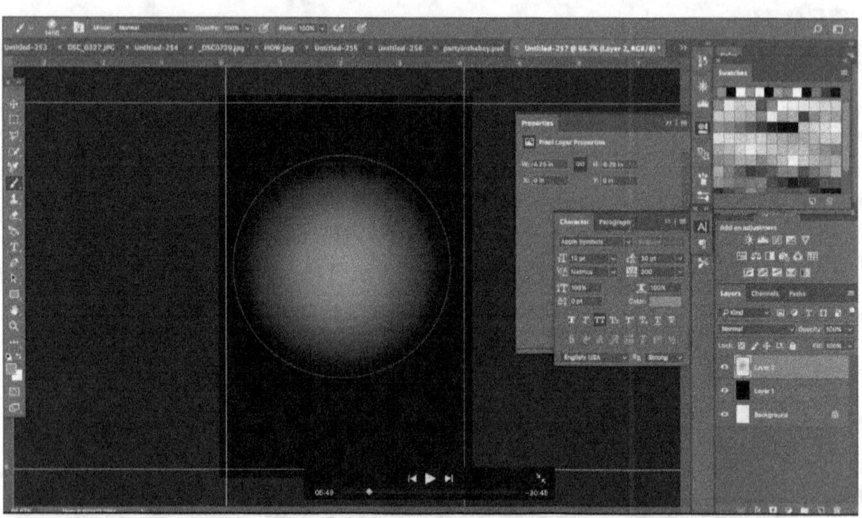

STEP 11

Now we are getting ready to move in toward the fun part. We are now going to create the white smudge in the background to make it look kind of like an abstract background

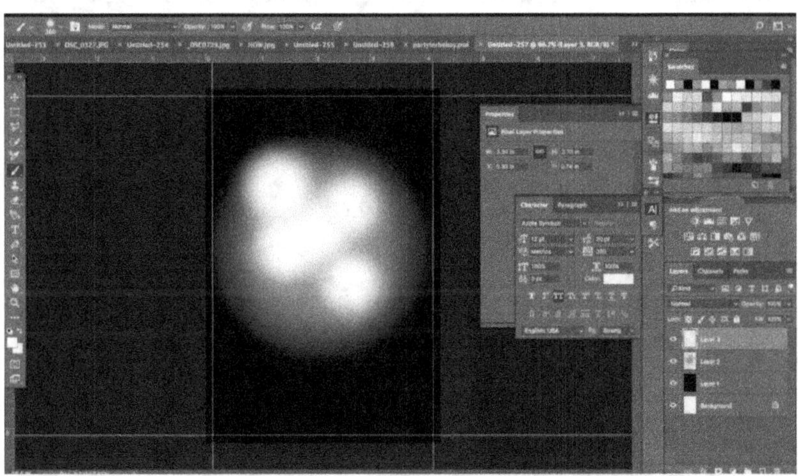

STEP 12

Next step you want to go to your tool bar and click the smudge tool. You have the freedom to choose which ever brush you want to use because there is not wrong or right way to this trick it's really about how creative your mind can get.

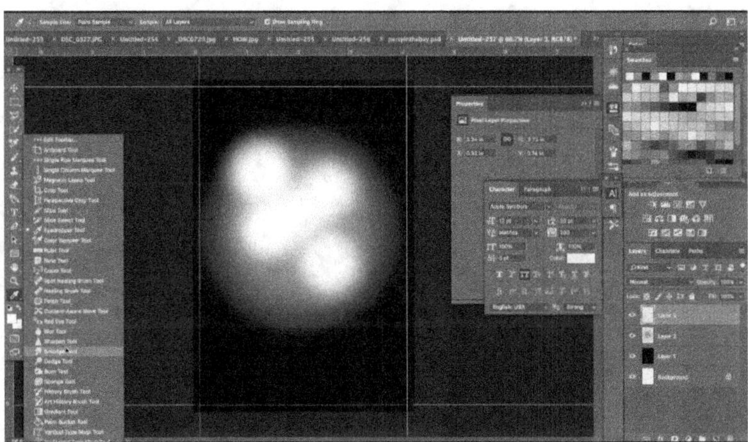

STEP 13

Next you will take your smudge brush and begin to wipe in the white soft air brush circles you have on the flyer. Which will start creating smudge lines in the background. Make sure the layer is selected that you did the white paint brush on. Otherwise you want see any results.

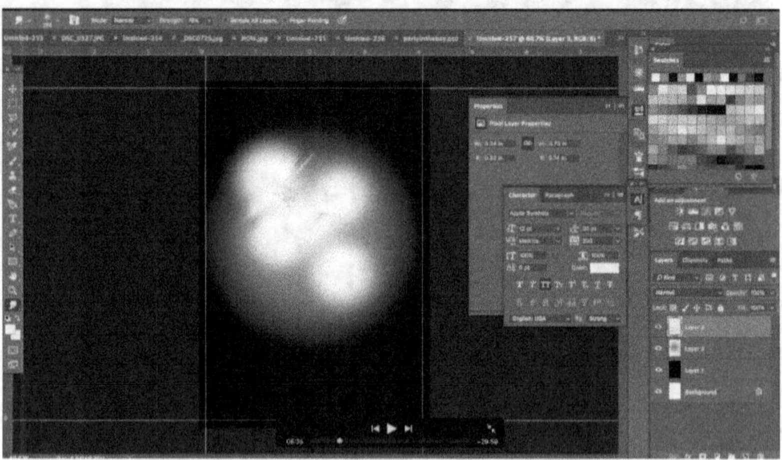

If you followed me step by step in the end you should have something like this or along the line with a smudge type of look to it.

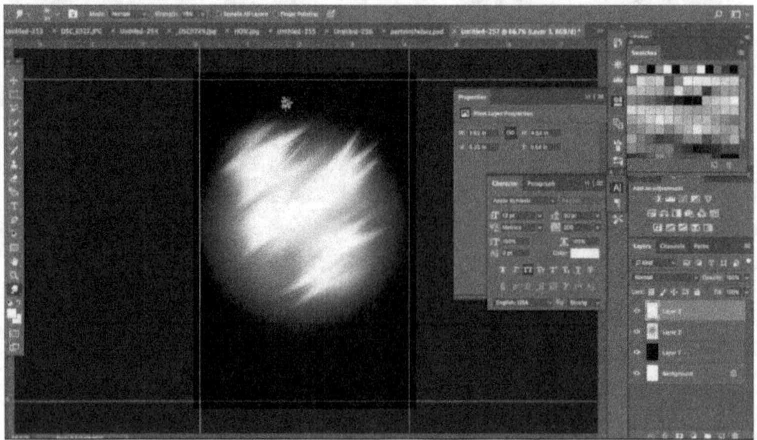

STEP 14:

We are now going to take the layer we made our white smudge on and turn it into an overlay. We are now going to go over to our layers box and click the box that says normal.

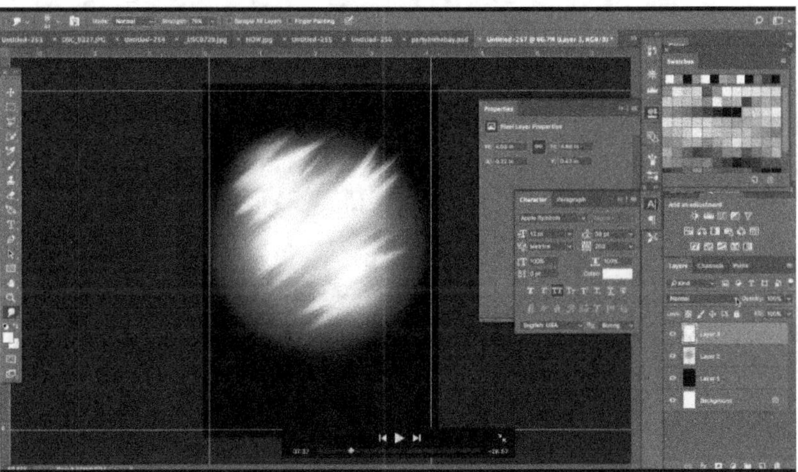

After we click the box that says normal scroll down and click on the word that says overlay.

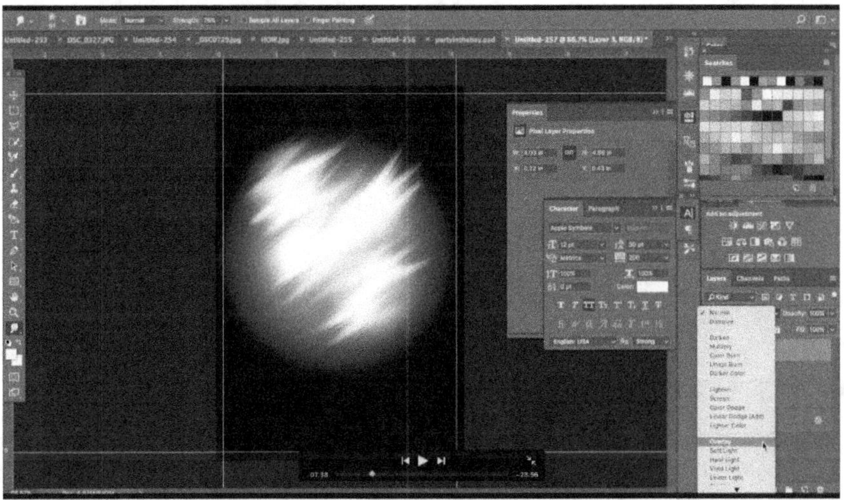

After you click overlay your smudge layer should look like this mine does in the picture below.

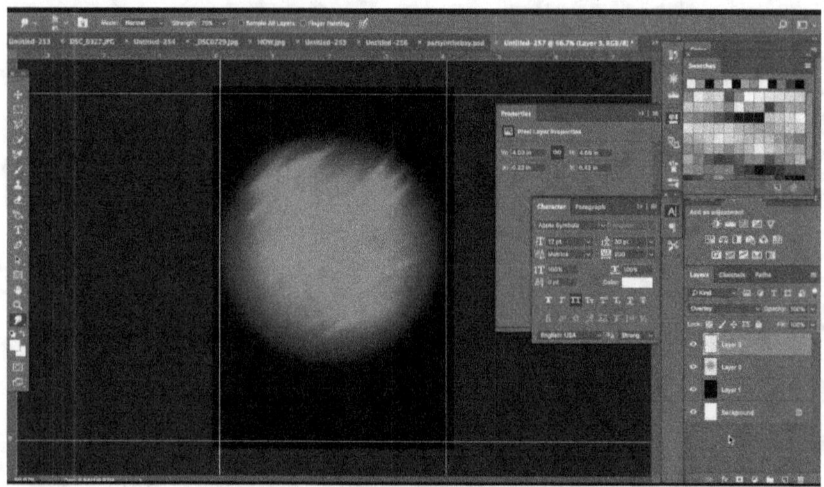

You have now completed the full setup for designing a flyer design as far as the bleeding points and the background

THIS IS A FULL BUS WRAP DESIGN I CREATED FOR A LARGE EVENT IN LAS VEGAS.

WORDS OF ENCOURAGEMENT

CASEY DIGGS | AUTHOR

I would like to thank everyone that supported me and purchased this book. As you read, I hope and pray that you received some useful information on which direction to go into when it comes time for the graphic design industry. Let this information sow into you and inspire you along your entrepreneurial journey. Remember there is nothing to hard or tough for you to achieve, because the sky is the limit. Continue to work hard, never give up, and always keep God first. Though all things that he has strengthen you, I can assure you that one day you will reach your full potential. If I can do it so can you.